SPACE WALK

Rob Waring, *Series Editor*

HEINLE
CENGAGE Learning™

Australia • Brazil • Japan • Korea • Mexico • Singapore • Spain • United Kingdom • United States

D0584524

Words to Know

This story talks about outer space, which is the area located beyond Earth's atmosphere.

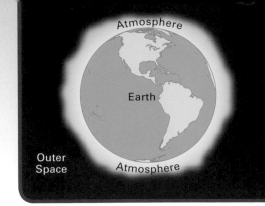

Atmosphere

Earth

Outer Space

Atmosphere

A **The Challenges of Space.** Read the paragraph. Then match each word or phrase with the correct definition.

Surviving in outer space creates a number of environmental challenges. On Earth we are kept in place by gravity, but in outer space gravity does not exist. There, humans become weightless and can float away if not connected to something solid. In addition, space is almost a perfect vacuum, empty of the precious oxygen we need to survive. It's also full of harmful radiation which can severely damage human tissue. Overall, the environment of space is extremely dangerous for humans without the protection of a space suit.

1. gravity _____

2. float _____

3. vacuum _____

4. radiation _____

5. tissue _____

6. space suit _____

a. protective clothing worn in space

b. a totally empty and airless space

c. powerful and sometimes dangerous waves of energy

d. rest or move slowly on water or in the air

e. a natural force pulling objects to the ground

f. a group of connected, similar cells that perform a certain function together

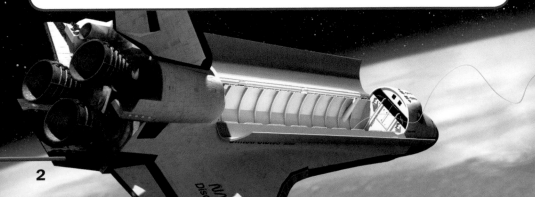

B Astronaut Training. Read the paragraph. Then write each underlined word or phrase next to the correct definition.

The National Aeronautics and Space Administration, or NASA, is a U.S. government agency that trains the nation's astronauts. These brave men and women must learn how to fly and live in spacecrafts, such as space shuttles. Before they leave on a mission, they must also get used to spending a lot of time in a weightless state while circling the Earth in orbit. Therefore, at the NASA laboratories, astronauts are sometimes immersed in water tanks for long periods to create a similar experience. Then, scientists measure the physiological effects of these experiments on their bodies in an effort to compute the effects of living in such an unusual environment.

1. people whose jobs include traveling and working in spacecrafts: _____
2. completely surrounded by something: _____
3. of or related to the way in which the body works: _____
4. moving along a curved path in space around a planet, moon, or star: _____
5. spacecrafts designed to travel between Earth and a space station: _____
6. a specific and important official task or job: _____

An Astronaut Floating in a Space Suit near the U.S. Space Shuttle

The view of the sky and Earth while in orbit looks beautifully calm but despite its peaceful appearance, the vacuum of space is a **hostile**[1] environment. Lacking oxygen and filled with radiation, if a human being were to step outside of a spacecraft without protection, he or she would experience any number of terrible physical damages. The person would become unconscious within seconds because of the lack of oxygen to the brain. The lack of air pressure would induce the blood and other liquids in the body to boil, which would also cause the expansion of the body's tissues. Temperature would also be a factor, with the astronaut possibly freezing or burning depending upon his or her location in relation to the sun. In addition, he or she would be exposed to radiation, which in large amounts can cause damage to any matter—particularly living tissue.

Human beings clearly cannot survive in such an unforgiving environment, yet people have been exploring the unfriendly frontier of space since manned space flights began in the 1960s. A number of brave astronauts have reached this seemingly impossible achievement with the help of spaceships, space suits, and other scientific inventions to help them endure the challenges of space. Through this modern technology, people have been able to explore the world beyond Earth's atmosphere.

[1]**hostile:** unfriendly or unwelcoming; opposing

CD 3, Track 01

Predict

Answer the questions. Then check your answers on pages 7 and 8.

1. What are two conditions that must be controlled in order to allow astronauts to walk in the hostile environment of space?

2. What temperature range must a space suit endure?

3. How many minutes did the first space walk last?

Given the extreme conditions, astronauts must wear specially designed space suits in order to survive in space. These space suits provide them with a self-contained environment to protect them when they risk leaving the safety of the spacecraft. The suits' tough material and heating and cooling elements protect astronauts from extreme temperatures which can range from around 121 degrees Celsius* to minus 157 degrees Celsius. The suits are also pressurized, which allows astronauts to breathe while in an environment without oxygen. This pressurization also keeps the air pressure around the astronauts' bodies normal and stops their blood from boiling in the vacuum of space.

* See page 24 for a metric conversion chart.

The first daring steps outside a spacecraft were made by Soviet astronaut **Aleksei Leonov**[2] on March 18, 1965. Leonov's historic walk took place on the Voskhod 2 flight. He was outside the spacecraft for 12 minutes, connected to the craft by only a short rope. His adventurous first space walk was not only exciting, but also dangerous. At the end of the short space walk, Leonov's space suit had filled out in the vacuum of space to the point where he could not reenter the **airlock**.[3] In the end, he had to open a **valve**[4] to allow some of the suit's pressure to escape, and was barely able to get back inside the spacecraft.

This space walking achievement was repeated a few months later by American astronaut Edward White. White took his first historic outing during the Gemini 4 mission, which first launched into space on June 3, 1965. On that same day, White became the first American to space walk, staying outside of the safety of the spacecraft for a total of 23 minutes.

---

[2]**Aleksei Leonov:** [ələksei lɪyɔnəf]
[3]**airlock:** a room between two areas that have different air pressure that allows a person to go from one area to the other, adjusting to the different pressures
[4]**valve:** a mechanism that opens and closes to stop or allow liquid or air to pass

Edward White (left) and James McDivitt (right) were members of the Gemini 4 mission.

Although these short trips were intended only to test the possibility of humans existing outside of spacecrafts, space walks have become a relatively common part of missions in the space shuttle **era**.[5] Space walks are essential for a number of reasons, but are important mainly due to the fact that on space walks, astronauts are able to perform crucial tasks that could not be accomplished from inside the shuttle. For example, astronauts have been able to recover lost **satellites**[6] and restore them to their proper orbit. They've serviced and repaired orbiting bodies, like replacing the **solar panels**[7] on the Hubble Space Telescope, which was carried into Earth's orbit by a space shuttle in April, 1990. Space walks have also enabled astronauts to form a construction team for the International Space Station, a research facility currently being put together in space.

---

[5]**era:** time period
[6]**satellite:** a human-made object that circles a larger one in space
[7]**solar panel:** a piece of equipment that collects energy from sunlight in order to produce electricity

The Hubble Space Telescope

Conducting space walks is not without challenges. Working in space suits is not as easy as one might think. The thick, pressurized gloves of the space suits make getting hold of tools difficult for the astronauts. The suits can also be uncomfortable when one spends long periods of time in them.

In addition, the weightlessness of space creates its own challenges. For the space-walking astronauts, there's always the constant danger of floating away into space due to the lack of gravity. Therefore, astronauts work in pairs, tied to the spacecraft for safety. While in space, liquids within the body are no longer affected by gravity, but the heart still operates as if it were on Earth. So rather than the body's blood being pulled into the legs, the pressure of the heart and **blood vessels**[8] often pushes the blood to the astronaut's body and head. This causes the **veins**[9] of the neck and face to stand out more than usual, and the eyes to become red and swollen. The astronauts may also suffer from headaches. This condition is known as 'puffy face **syndrome**'[10] because the face often appears puffy, or swollen.

---

[8]**blood vessels:** any of many blood-carrying tubes that bring blood to the heart and lungs
[9]**vein:** a blood vessel that carries blood to the heart
[10]**syndrome:** condition; illness

Puffy face syndrome is not the only illness that these adventurers must face, particularly when considering the physiological changes that can be induced when living in space for some period of time. Astronauts can also suffer from illnesses such as 'space sickness' or 'space adaptation syndrome.' About 40 percent of those people who have gone into space have experienced **dizziness**[11] or **nausea**[12] at some point. Fortunately, these types of sicknesses aren't long-lasting or permanent in any way. They generally wear off after two or three days spent back on Earth, as soon as the astronaut's body has had time to readapt to Earth's gravitational pull and atmosphere.

---

[11] **dizziness:** a feeling that everything is moving around, and that you are not able to balance
[12] **nausea:** a feeling of sickness in the stomach

To ensure space walk missions are successful, astronauts have to practice for their planned walks, often for quite some time. Leonov, for example, spent years going through intense training before he went on his mission in 1965.

Nowadays, astronauts practice at a special NASA laboratory where weightlessness is studied in detail. They are sent into a large water-filled tank and remain there for long periods of time in order to test the physiological effects of living in a weightless environment such as space. While they are immersed in the water, the astronauts neither sink nor float, creating a sensation close to weightlessness. For every hour of tasks scheduled on a mission, up to ten hours are spent practicing underwater. It also gives the astronauts an opportunity to experience life in the thick protective suits in which they'll be living, working, and 'hanging out' for much of the time while in space.

Infer Meaning

1. What does the phrase 'wear off' on page 15 mean? Look at the words around it and write a definition.

2. What two meanings does the phrase 'hang out' on page 16 have? Look at the words around it and write definitions for both the literal and slang uses of the expression.

Such demanding practice schedules and training are obviously hard on the human body, and require extremely high levels of fitness. There is no doubt that space walks bring challenges to the astronauts who have to do them, but as NASA moves forward on the maintenance and construction of the International Space Station, space walks will continue to be essential to the process. The project, which began construction in 1998, has a projected operations date through at least 2016. By that time, workers will have completed the station and it will likely be totally operational. Considering this and other possible space projects, it looks like there will be plenty of work to keep space walkers busy for quite some time to come.

After You Read

1. Each of the following is an example of why space is a hostile environment EXCEPT:
   A. extremely high air pressure
   B. vast temperature differences
   C. radiation
   D. no oxygen

2. What's the meaning of 'self-contained' on page 7?
   A. neutral
   B. automatic
   C. separate
   D. ambiguous

3. What nationality was the first person who walked in space?
   A. American
   B. Japanese
   C. Russian
   D. British

4. What was the purpose of the 1965 space walks?
   A. to recover a lost satellite
   B. to see if the human body could survive in space
   C. to test a new kind of spacecraft
   D. to replace solar panels on a telescope

5. What is the International Space Station?
   A. an orbiting telescope
   B. a place for space research
   C. a location to practice space walks
   D. a training facility on Earth

6. According to the writer, why is working in a space suit difficult?
   A. The heat of the suit can make one's blood boil.
   B. A suit may sometimes start to leak.
   C. The air inside a space suit is freezing.
   D. An astronaut's mobility is limited.

7. The writer implies that astronauts work in pairs in space because:
   A. One may float out into space.
   B. One might faint.
   C. They need to tie each other's ropes.
   D. Space can be very lonely.

8. On page 15, 'they' refers to:
   A. the illnesses
   B. the space walks
   C. the astronauts
   D. NASA

9. Most illnesses in space happen because the human body:
   A. reacts differently to the environment in outer space
   B. adapts too quickly to the space suits
   C. tries to preserve itself by getting sick
   D. swells from the pressure on the heart

10. If an astronaut spent 40 hours practicing underwater, how long is their task on the mission?
    A. 1 hour
    B. 2 hours
    C. 4 hours
    D. 40 hours

11. Astronauts must test the physiological effects of living in _____ weightless environment by practicing underwater.
    A. an
    B. a
    C. one
    D. some

12. What does the writer imply about space walks in the final paragraph?
    A. NASA needs to design a better space suit.
    B. Space walks are too dangerous for humans to do.
    C. It's not fair that astronauts have to go on space walks.
    D. Space walks are a necessary part of space exploration.

Class:	Science
Teacher:	Mr. Hutchinson
Assignment:	Write a short report about a future space discovery.

Vacationing in Space

Commercial airlines began to investigate the idea of sending people on vacations in outer space as early as 1968. During the Apollo 8 space exploration flight, astronauts sent back space images that were then shown on television. During a break in the program, Pan American Airways announced that they would begin accepting reservations for commercial passenger flights to the moon, which would begin as soon as they became practical. Obviously, Pan Am hasn't made the flight yet, but the idea raised some interesting questions: who could finance the development of this private space travel, how soon could the technology be ready, and how could passengers' safety be guaranteed?

Apollo 11 begins its flight to the moon on July 16, 1969.

Finance

Space travel is extremely expensive, and it soon became clear that the only entities with enough money and interest to conduct the necessary research and development were the governments of certain countries. Funding for the programs fluctuated over the years, partly because of economic issues. Then, in 2001 an American businessman named Dennis Tito was able to take advantage of the Russian space program's need for help offsetting its costs. He was able to buy himself a visit to the International Space Station for seven days, traveling aboard a Russian spacecraft. He is said to have paid a sum of US $20 million for the privilege.

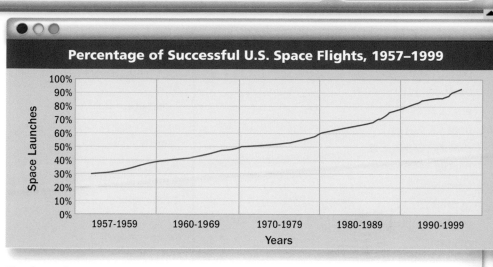

Percentage of Successful U.S. Space Flights, 1957–1999

Space Launches (y-axis): 0% to 100%

Years (x-axis): 1957-1959, 1960-1969, 1970-1979, 1980-1989, 1990-1999

Technology

Although both the airlines and potential passengers have remained committed to the idea, private sector development has been very slow. Recently, however, the investment in research and development has begun to pay off. In June 2004, 'SpaceShipOne,' the first privately developed manned flight, was launched from the Mojave Desert in California. The launch was attended by a large group of scientists, business people, and movie stars. The company plans to build more ships and to begin offering commercial flights sometime in the future under the name 'Virgin Galactic.'

Safety

The final issue remains: is space flight really a safe undertaking for relatively untrained people? According to Virgin Galactic's website, their planes are carefully designed and will be thoroughly tested before commercial flights begin. Passengers will be required to have physical exams and take a three-day training program before launch. However, there is always an element of risk. Of the 4,378 space launches conducted worldwide between 1957 and 1999, 390 launches failed. The ratio of successful launches to unsuccessful launches has increased over the years, but prospective passengers should consider the statistics carefully before signing up for a space vacation.

CD 3, Track 02

Word Count: 403
Time: _____

Vocabulary List

airlock (8)
astronaut (3, 4, 5, 7, 8, 11, 12, 15, 16, 19)
blood vessel (12)
dizziness (15)
era (11)
float (2, 12, 16)
gravity (2, 12, 15)
hostile (4, 5)
immerse (3, 16)
in orbit (3, 11)
mission (3, 8, 11, 16)
nausea (15)
physiological (3, 15, 16)
radiation (2, 4)
satellite (11)
solar panel (11)
space shuttle (3, 11)
space suit (2, 4, 7, 8, 12)
syndrome (12, 15)
tissue (2, 4)
vacuum (2, 4, 7, 8)
valve (8)
vein (12)

Metric Conversion Chart

Area
1 hectare = 2.471 acres

Length
1 centimeter = .394 inches
1 meter = 1.094 yards
1 kilometer = .621 miles

Temperature
0° Celsius = 32° Fahrenheit

Volume
1 liter = 1.057 quarts

Weight
1 gram = .035 ounces
1 kilogram = 2.2 pounds